SIGHTSINGING
THE COMPLETE METHOD FOR SINGERS

by Mike Campbell

ISBN 978-0-7935-8191-7

7777 W. BLUEMOUND RD. P.O. BOX 13819 MILWAUKEE, WI 53213

Visit Hal Leonard Online at
www.halleonard.com

Acknowledgments

I want to take this opportunity to thank all the teachers, musicians, and singers who have shared their knowledge and experience with me through the years. I have had the privilege to study and work with some of the most incredible and giving people in the world. A very special thanks to Lee and Sally Sweetland, Ted Greene, Fletcher Peck, Abby Fraser, George Wilkins, Jack Smalley, Alf Clausen, and—last but not least—Tom Garvin, who has been an inspirational musical partner, teacher, friend, and my arranger for over twenty-five years.

I also want to thank all my students over the years who have inspired and challenged me. They have consistently shown me that we have to take risks to grow in our life and in our music. They make me laugh, and they make me crazy—but most of all, they make me feel. I am a lucky man!

This book is dedicated to my family: my wife Elaine and my daughters Katie and Megan, who are my three favorite singers in the world; my mom and dad, who paid for lessons, whose love was unconditional, and who always encouraged me and never asked me when I would get a real job; and my brother Dudley, his wife Candy, and daughter Tiffany, who are always there with love and food, and who do ask me when I'm going to get a real job.

Table of Contents

Introduction

This book is designed for the singer who has no background in reading music. It is my hope that with consistent work habits and patience, you will develop a strong foundation in reading rhythms and sightsinging melodies. Knowing how to read music may not turn you into a great singer, but it will give you the confidence you need to improve as a singer. This knowledge will help you learn songs faster, ease your fear of other musicians finding out that you know nothing about music, improve your musical ears, and turn you into a singer/musician who knows his or her craft.

Learning to read music is not very difficult if you organize your time and practice the exercises every day. Each chapter in this book begins with exercises in rhythm, then in sightsinging and/or ear training. *Always use a metronome when practicing.* Try to get together with other singers to practice in small groups and *help each other!* It's more fun working with friends but sometimes it's just you and your piano (or keyboard). One of the most important keys to sightsinging is simply reading through lots of material, so there are many exercises in this book to sing through. *Do the work!* Nothing is ever gained without hard work—but don't forget to have fun!

—*Mike Campbell*

Chapter One

Getting Started

This book is based on the assumption that you have no previous experience with reading music. The format will include clapping out and singing rhythms. The objective of this first section is to teach you how to read rhythms.

Rhythm and Beat

Probably the most fundamental component of rhythm is the *beat,* the pulse found in most music. The beat is that to which you dance, clap your hands, or tap your foot. The beat remains basically steady—like a heartbeat. The beat and rhythm are not one and the same. Rhythm is a larger concept, including the beat and everything that happens to sounds in relation to time.

Meter and Tempo

Although beats in music are evenly spaced, some receive special emphasis. In music, some beats receive more emphasis than others. These beats are called *accented beats.* If one beat in every two is accented, the listener feels the rhythm like this: *Beat–beat–Beat–beat.* If the accent is once every three beats, the listener feels: *Beat–beat–beat–Beat–beat–beat.* The beats occur evenly in these cases and have a pattern. The pattern is called *meter.*

The word *tempo* in refers to the rate of speed at which the beat occurs; it is the pace of the beat.

Measures and Bar Lines

The horizontal and divided spaces on the staff are called *measures;* the vertical lines are called *bar lines.*

Notes

The *note* is the symbol that is placed on the staff to indicate which musical pitch you are to sing, and how long and when you are to sing it. The position of the note on the staff determines its pitch. The duration is shown by the construction of the note.

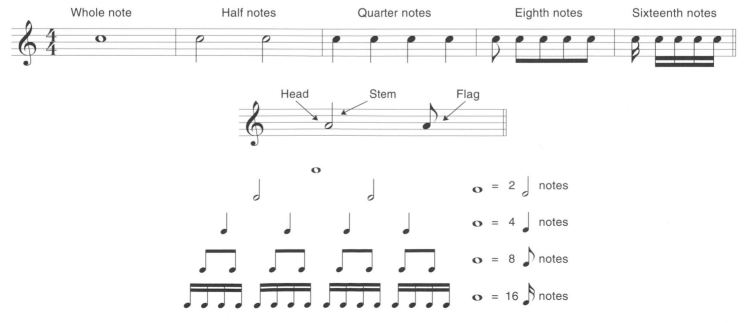

Rests

Rests are like notes; they have specific time values and a definite way of being written. The big difference is that rests indicate silence rather than sound.

Time Signatures

Each measure of music has a certain number of beats in it. The number of beats per measure and the kind of note getting one beat is determined by a sign at the beginning of the music called a *time signature.* The time signature is written as one number above another; 4/4 is an example of a time signature. The bottom number tells you what kind of note gets one beat; the top note tells you how many beats there will be in a measure. For instance, the top "4" equals four beats per measure, while the bottom "4" means a quarter note gets one beat.

Whatever the time signature says *must be* contained in each measure. The number of beats in a measure can be made up of any combination of notes and rests, as long as there is the correct number of beats.

Since 4/4 is the most common time signature, it is often referred to as *common time.* This is symbolized by a "C" where you would normally see "4/4," though they both mean the same thing. Study this figure carefully!

Ties

A *tie* is a curved line connecting *two notes of the same pitch.* When you see a tie, you play the first note only, and hold the sound for the length of both notes.

Dots

The *dot* is a device used to increase any note by half its own value. For instance, a quarter note is equal to two eighth notes and a quarter note with a dot after it is equal to three eighth notes.

EXERCISE: Time Signatures

The following are some examples of time signatures. Analyze each one, and write the correct description below.

1. _4 BEATS PER MEASURE – QUARTER NOTE GETS ONE BEAT_

2. _____

3. _____

4. _____

5. _____

6. _____

7. _____

8. _____

9. _____

10. _____

Subdividing the Beat

If you have 4/4 time and four quarter notes in a measure, each note gets one beat and gets all of that beat. However, it is possible to divide the beat up into smaller parts. If two eighth notes equal one quarter note, then in a measure of 4/4 you could substitute two eighth notes for every one quarter note.

To divide the beat up and count it out loud, you would say "one–and, two–and, three– and, four–and."

In this chapter, we have discussed musical time as it relates to both rhythm and meter. Remember, rhythm is the duration of pitch and silence in music; meter is rhythm measured into regular recurrent beats. We will now start with some simple rhythm exercises.

Beginning Rhythm Exercises

Clap and count out loud:

The Major Scale

C Major

A major scale is composed of the following sequence of whole and half steps: whole-whole-half-whole-whole-whole-half. The scale below, C major, begins and ends with the note C, which is its key note. The key note is called the *tonic* and is where the key takes its name from. All major scales have a half step between the third and fourth steps of the scale and the seventh and eighth steps of the scale.

C major scale

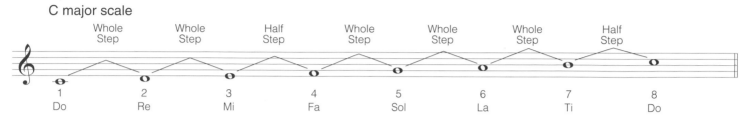

Sharps and Flats

Some scales, and therefore some key signatures, have *sharps* (♯) or *flats* (♭). The key of C has no sharps or flats. However, following the major scale pattern from on the note F requires the use of one flat (B♭), to preserve the half step between the third and fourth steps of the scale—from A to B♭.

F major scale

Similarly, the following scale starting on the note G has an F♯ because of the pattern's half step between the seventh and eighth steps of the scale.

G major scale

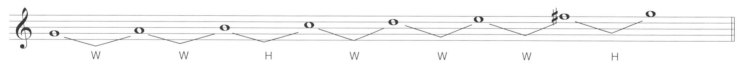

Let's start our sightsinging by singing the eight notes of a C major scale with the numbers 1–7.

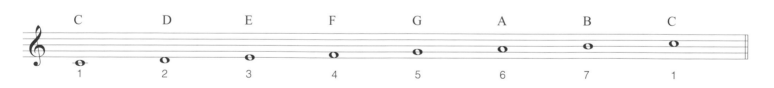

After practicing this a few times, move on to the following exercises. Here we'll use note values both in 4/4 and 3/4 time in the keys of C, F, and G.

Sightsinging

Sing through each of the following scales using numbers. For scales 6–15, fill in the key of each scale.

1 Key of C

Ear Training

For each example, play through the line first, and then sing it.

Chapter Two

2

Recognizing Patterns

To avoid confusion when you are first learning to read rhythms, you can count them out loud. This is a professional technique often used when there is a difficult measure of music. In Chapter 1, we saw how we will count "*One*–and, *two*–and, *three*–and, *four*–and," etc., counting each individual beat and rest, but we also want to start recognizing rhythmic *patterns.* It is impossible to count out every beat as you play and sing, especially at fast tempos. You must start to recognize the patterns.

Read and count through all the following examples. See how many patterns you can find within them.

Hearing What You See

One of the most important things in learning to sightsing is developing your ear so you can hear what your eyes see in the music. Your ear must be trained to hear the difference between the intervals.

INTERVAL WARM-UPS

Singing through the following examples will help develop your ear *and* get you warmed up! Notice the number of half steps within each interval.

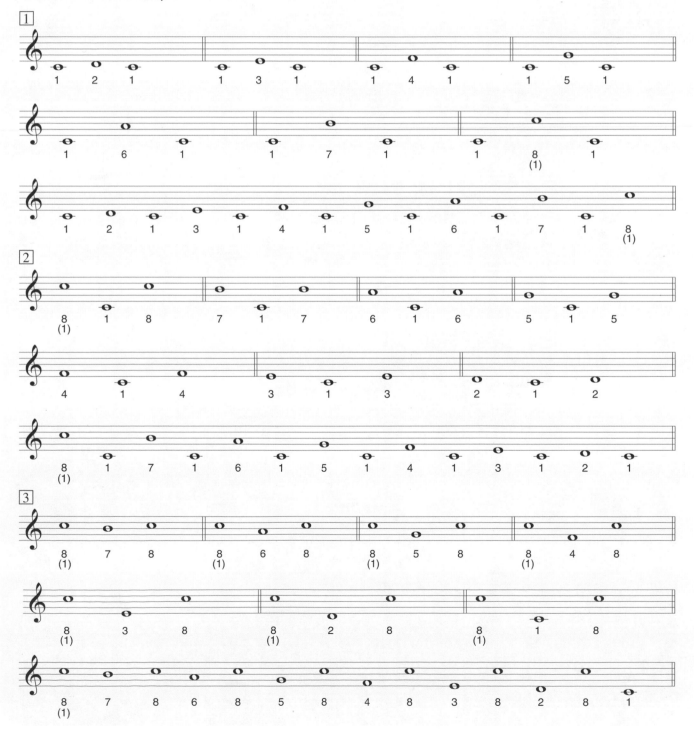

Sightsinging—Simple Melodies

In this chapter, we will start with the first five notes of the major scale, then expand.

Ear Training

For each example, play through the line first and then sing it.

Chapter Three

Ties

We will begin Chapter 3 by getting more familiar with ties. A tie joins two notes together. If you need to refresh your memory, go back to Chapter 1 and reread the segment on ties.

Clap and/or sing the following exercises:

INTERVAL WARM-UPS

Sing each exercise four times using the numbers without using an instrument. Afterwards, check yourself on a keyboard to make sure you're singing the notes correctly.

Ear Training

For each example, first play through the scale and then the exercise. Listen, and then sing it.

Key of C

1. 1 1 2 1
2. 1 3 2 1
3. 1 4 3 2 1
4. 1 3 2 3 1

5. 1 2 3 4 1
6. 1 5 4 3 1
7. 3 4 5 6 7 1
8. 1 3 5 6 5

Key of F

9. 1 3 2 1
10. 1 2 3 4 3
11. 1 1 3 3 1
12. 1 3 5 3 1

13. 1 5 5 1
14. 1 2 3 2 3
15. 1 5 4 3 1
16. 1 2 1 2 3

Key of G

17. 1 3 1
18. 1 2 3 4 5
19. 1 3 5 4 3
20. 1 3 2 3 1

21. 1 3 5 6 5
22. 1 2 3 4 3
23. 1 5 1 3 1
24. 3 1 3 3 1

Sightsinging—Melodies in C, F, and G Major

The following phrases are in the keys of C, F, and G. Remember: always try to make each phrase as musical as possible.

1. 1 2 3 4 5 6 5 6 5 4 3 2 1

2. 1 2 3 4 5 6 5 4 3 2 1

3. 1 2 3 4 5 6 5 4 3 4 5 4 3 2 1

Chapter Four

4

Dotted Notes

We will begin Chapter 4 by getting more familiar with dots. You may recall from Chapter 1 that a dot adds half a note's length to itself.

Clap and/or sing the following exercises:

Sixteenth Notes

It's time now to get comfortable with sixteenth notes. As we saw in Chapter 1, four sixteenth notes equal one beat; you have four (4) claps in the space of one beat. We count them: "one–e–and–a."

Clap and/or sing the following exercises:

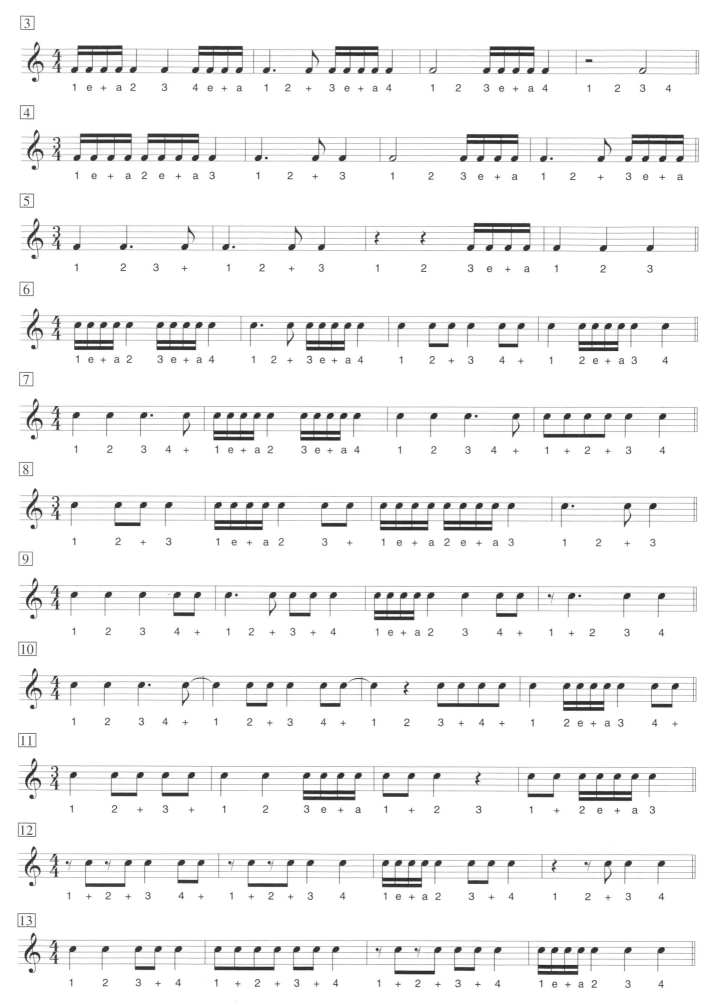

INTERVAL WARM-UPS

Name and sing the following intervals:

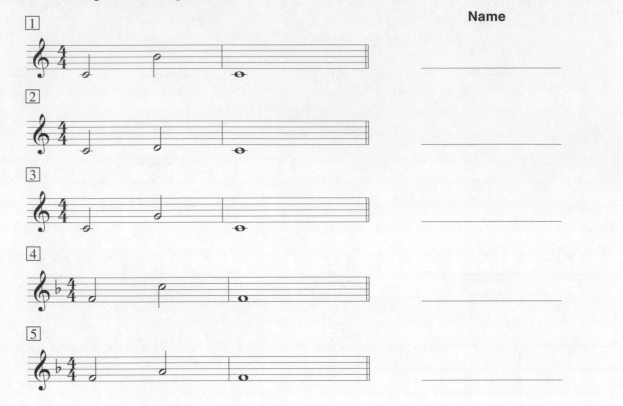

Ear Training

For each example, first play through the scale and then the exercise. Listen, and then sing it.

Key of B♭

Sightsinging—Melodies in C, F, G, and B♭ Major

The following phrases are in the keys of C, F, G, and B♭. Be conscious of each interval you sing.

Chapter Five

5

Combining Dotted Notes and Sixteenth Notes

Clap and/or sing the following exercises:

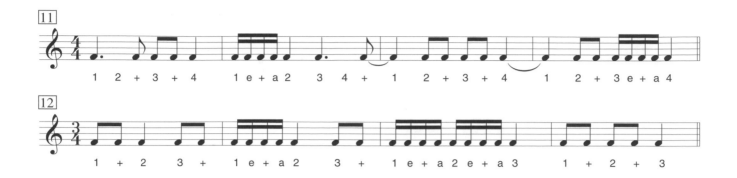

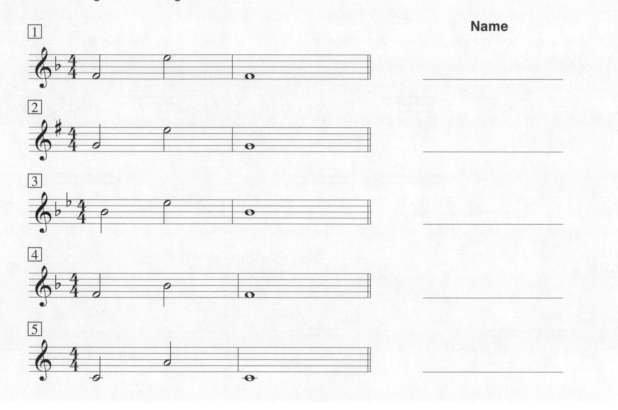

INTERVAL WARM-UPS

Name and sing the following intervals:

Name

Ear Training

For each example, first play through the scale and then the exercise. Listen, and then sing it.

Key of C

1. 1 3 5 4 1
2. 5 6 7 2 1
3. 5 3 5 7 1
4. 1 1 5 7 1

Key of F

5. 1 3 1 5 1
6. 5 4 3 7 1
7. 2 2 3 5 1
8. 1 1 7 6 5

Key of G

Key of B♭

Key of D

Sightsinging—Melodies in C, F, G, B♭, and D Major

The following phrases are in the keys of C, F, G, B♭, and D. Be conscious of each interval you sing.

Introducing the Bass Clef

Now let's take a look at the bass clef. Notice that the C on the ledger line *above* the bass clef is the same C as the C on the ledger line below the treble clef.

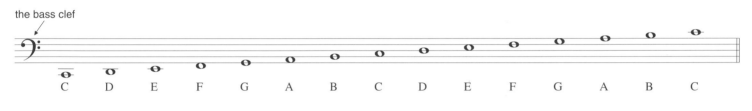

Sing through the following bass clef phrases:

Chapter Six

6

Combining Eighths and Sixteenths

In music notation, you will find often that note lengths can be written more than one way. Below are some examples of rhythms written differently but sounding the same.

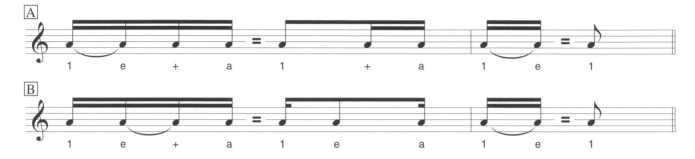

These rhythms can be written either way and be correct. However, the second way in each example is more common.

Clap and/or sing the following exercises:

Triplets

So far we have become familiar singing one note per beat (quarter note), two notes per beat (eighth notes), and four notes per beat (sixteenth notes). But what about three notes per beat? When you divide a beat into three equal parts, it is called a *triplet.*

Clap and/or sing the following exercises:

INTERVAL WARM-UPS

Name and sing the following intervals:

Name

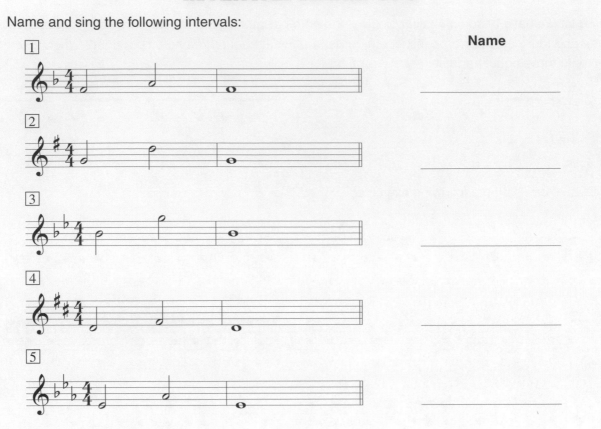

Ear Training

For each example, first play through the scale and then the exercise. Listen, and then sing it.

Sightsinging—Melodies in C, F, G, B♭, D, and E♭ Major

The following phrases are in the keys of C, F, G, B♭, D, and E♭.

Sightsinging in the Bass Clef

Sing through the following bass clef phrases:

Chapter Seven

7

Combining Dotted Eighths and Sixteenths

Below is another "sounds alike" example:

Clap and/or sing the following exercises:

INTERVAL WARM-UPS

Name and sing the following intervals:

Name

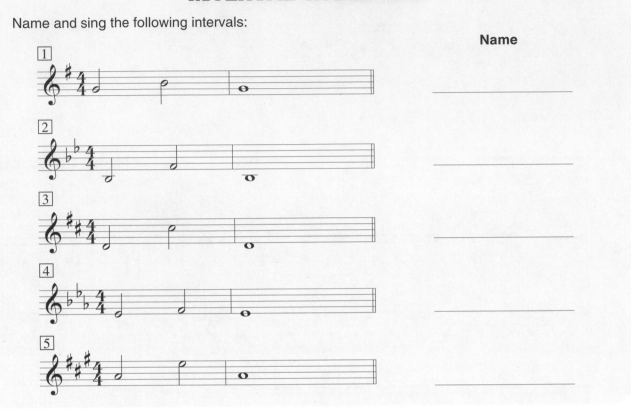

Ear Training

For each example, first play through the scale and then the exercise. Listen, and then sing it.

Sightsinging—Melodies in C, F, G, B♭, D, E♭, and A Major

The following phrases are in the keys of C, F, G, B♭, D, E♭, and A.

Sightsinging in the Bass Clef

Sing through the following bass clef phrases:

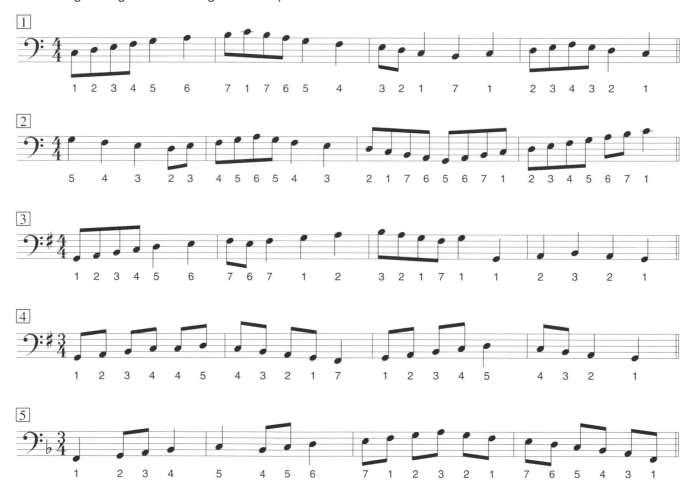

Chapter Eight

8

Cut Time

Cut time is indicated by a "C" with a slash through it. Cut time is equivalent to 2/2 time.

$$\mathbf{C} = \frac{4}{4} \quad \text{In } \frac{4}{4}, \text{ we feel four beats per measure.}$$

$$\mathbf{\mathbb{C}} = \frac{2}{2} \quad \text{In } \frac{2}{2}, \text{ we feel two beats per measure.}$$

Clap and/or sing the following cut time exercises:

Combining Note Values

These exercises focus on sixteenth notes, dotted notes, eighth notes, and tied notes.

INTERVAL WARM-UPS

Start with the root (1) of each key. Write out the intervals, then sing them.

M = major   m = minor   P = perfect

D = diminished   A = augmented

Ear Training

For each example, first play through the scale and then the exercise. Listen, and then sing it.

Sightsinging—Melodies in C, F, G, B♭, D, E♭, A, A♭, E, and D♭ Major

The following phrases are in the keys of C, F, G, B♭, D, E♭, A, A♭, E, and D♭. (Watch the clefs.)

Chapter Nine

9

6/8 Time

In 6/8 time, there are six beats in each measure, and an eighth note gets one beat. However, 6/8 time is usually felt in two (instead of six), with the strong beats falling on 1 and 4 and the weak beats falling on 2, 3, 5, and 6.

6 = six counts in a measure
8 = eighth note gets one count

Clap and/or sing the following exercises:

Combining Note Values

Clap and/or sing the following exercises:

INTERVAL WARM-UPS

Name and sing the following intervals:

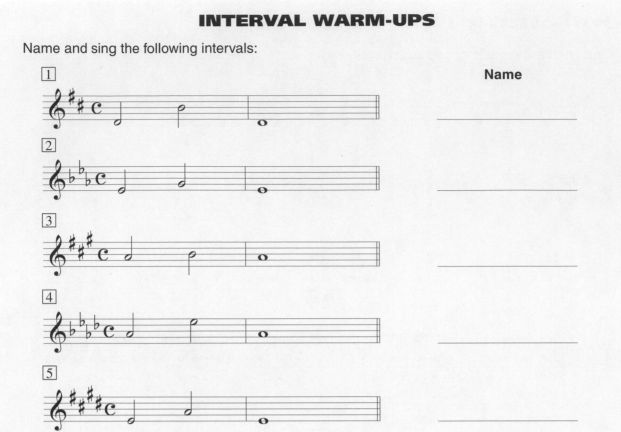

Name

1 _____

2 _____

3 _____

4 _____

5 _____

Ear Training

For each example, first play through the scale and then the exercise, listen, and then sing it.

Sightsinging—Melodies in C, F, G, B♭, D, E♭, A, A♭, E, D♭, B, G♭, F♯, C♭, and C♯ Major

The following phrases are in the keys of C, F, G, B♭, D, E♭, A, A♭, E, D♭, B, G♭, F♯, C♭, and C♯.

10

5 5 6 5 1 7 6 7 1 2 3 4 5 4 3 3 2 1

11

1 2 3 4 5 1 2 3 4 3 2 1 7 6 7 1

12

1 7 6 5 6 7 1 3 2 3 4 5 6 5 4 3 6 7 1

13

1 2 3 4 5 6 7 1 7 6 5 4 3 2 1 2 3 4 3 2 7 1

14

1 3 2 1 2 3 4 5 4 3 2 7 1 2 1

15

3 4 5 6 5 4 3 4 5 6 7 1 2 3 2 1 7 6 7 1

16

5 4 5 4 3 2 1 2 3 4 5 6 7 1 2 3 2 1

17

3 4 5 6 5 4 3 2 1 7 1 2 1

18

5 4 3 2 1 7 6 7 1 7 1

Chapter Ten

10

In this chapter, we will review all the material covered up to this point.

Rhythm—Review

Clap and/or sing the following exercises:

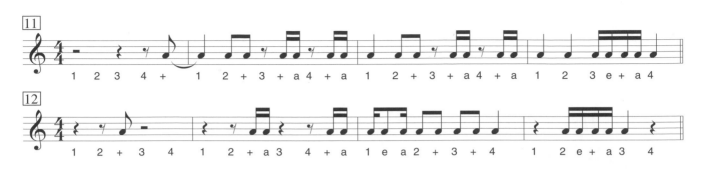

INTERVAL WARM-UPS

Name and sing the following intervals:

Name

Ear Training

For each example, first play through the scale and then the exercise. Listen, and then sing it.

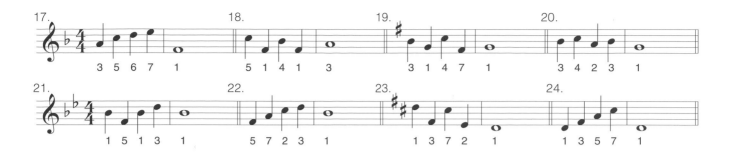

Sightsinging—Review

Sing through the following phrases:

11 Chapter Eleven

Mixed Rhythms

Clap and/or sing the following exercises:

Intervals and Their Inversions

All intervals can be inverted. For instance, if C up to D♭ is a minor second ascending, then C down to D♭ is a major seventh descending.

P1	m2	M2	m3	M3	P4	A4
↕	↕	↕	↕	↕	↕	↕
P8	M7	m7	M6	m6	P5	d5

INTERVAL WARM-UPS

Complete and sing (ascending intervals):

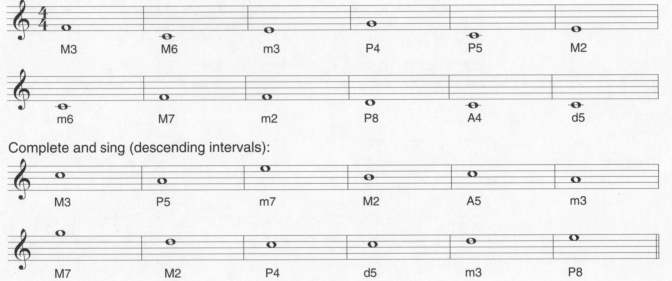

M3	M6	m3	P4	P5	M2
m6	M7	m2	P8	A4	d5

Complete and sing (descending intervals):

M3	P5	m7	M2	A5	m3
M7	M2	P4	d5	m3	P8

Sightsinging in Thirds

Sing the following phrases, which emphasize minor and major thirds.

1
1 3 2 4 3 5 4 6 5 7 6 1 7 2 1

2
3 1 2 7 1 6 7 5 6 4 5 3 4 2 3 1

3
1 2 3 1 2 3 4 3 4 5

4
1 3 5 3 4 2 3 1 2 4 3 1 3 5

Ear Training

For each example, first play through the scale and then the exercise. Listen, and then sing it.

Key of B♭

13.   14.   15.   16.

2 1 2 7 1   5 1 6 2 1   3 5 2 5 1   5 6 7 6 1

Key of D

17.   18.   19.   20.

3 5 7 2 3   1 5 3 6 5   7 6 5 4 5   1 1 5 3 1

Sightsinging—Major Melodies

Sing through the following phrases:

1

1   5 6 7   1   7   6   5   4   3   2   1

2

5   4   3   2   5   1   5   6 7 1   2   5   1

3

1   3   2   1   2   3   4   5   6   7 1 2   3   2   1

4

1   2   3   4   3   5 4 3   2   1 2 3   4   5 4 3 4 5   1

5

1   5   4   3   2   5   1   7   1   2   5   6   7   2   1

6

5   6 7 1   2   3   2   1   2   5   4   3   2 1 7   2   1

7

3   5   4   5   6 7 5   4   3   2   7   1   2   1

8

5   4   5   3   1   7   1   2   3   2   1 7   1

9

1   2   3   4   5   4 3   1   7   6   5   6   7 1

Chapter Twelve

12

Mixed Rhythms

Clap and/or sing the following exercises:

INTERVAL WARM-UPS

Complete and sing (ascending intervals):

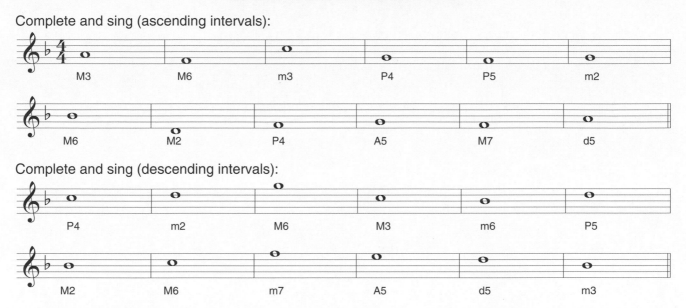

Complete and sing (descending intervals):

Triads and Arpeggios

By now you've probably heard about *chords.* But what are chords, and what are they made of? Three or more notes sounded together constitute a chord. The simplest chords are built from *triads.* A triad is a three-note chord made up of thirds. There are four types of triads: a *major triad* has a major third on bottom and a minor third on top; a *minor triad* has a minor third on bottom and a major third on top; a *diminished triad* has two minor thirds; and an *augmented triad* has two major thirds. The name of the triad is taken from the bottom note.

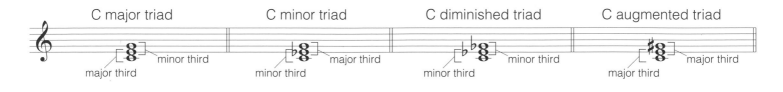

It is not possible to sing a triad (unless you have several different throats!). But it is possible to sing an *arpeggio.* When you play or sing the individual notes of a chord (or triad) one at a time, you are playing or singing an arpeggio.

Ear Training

Let's try singing some arpeggiated triads. For each example, first play through the exercise, listen, and then sing it.

Major

Sightsinging—Major Melodies

Sing through the following phrases:

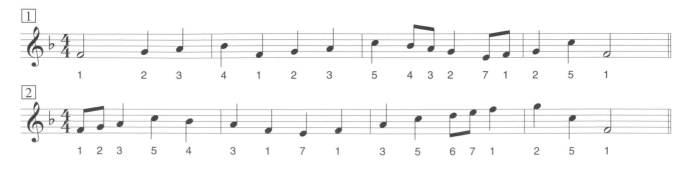

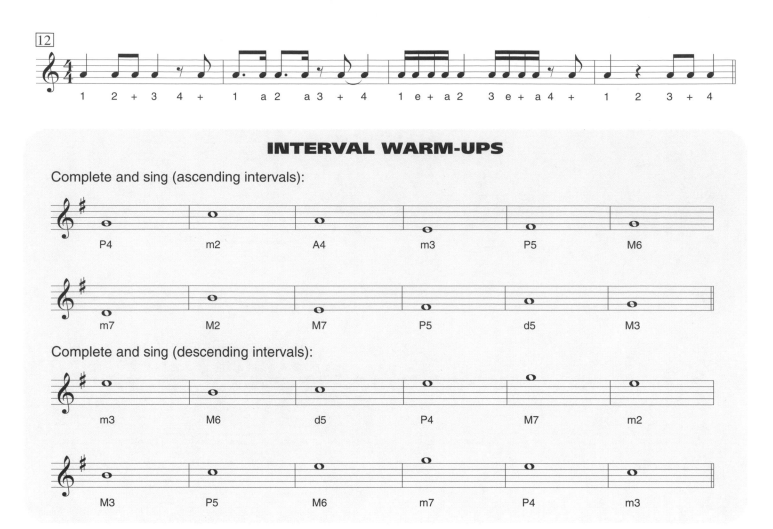

INTERVAL WARM-UPS

Complete and sing (ascending intervals):

| P4 | m2 | A4 | m3 | P5 | M6 |

| m7 | M2 | M7 | P5 | d5 | M3 |

Complete and sing (descending intervals):

| m3 | M6 | d5 | P4 | M7 | m2 |

| M3 | P5 | M6 | m7 | P4 | m3 |

Ear Training

For each example, first play through the exercise, listen, and then sing it.

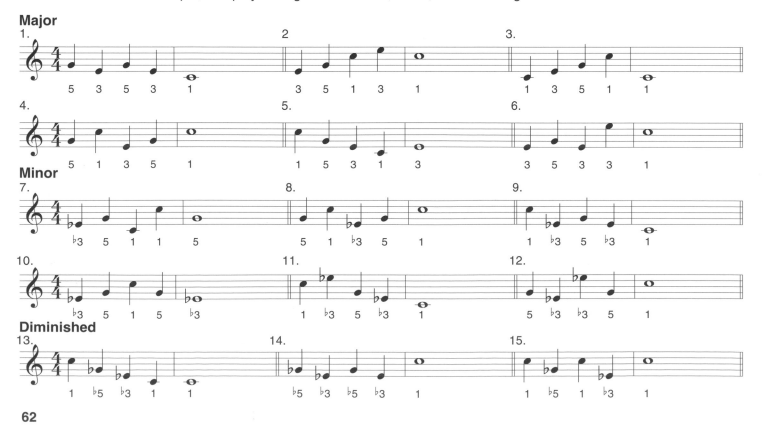

Major

1.
5 3 5 3 1

2.
3 5 1 3 1

3.
1 3 5 1 1

4.
5 1 3 5 1

5.
1 5 3 1 3

6.
3 5 3 3 1

Minor

7.
♭3 5 1 1 5

8.
5 1 ♭3 5 1

9.
1 ♭3 5 ♭3 1

10.
♭3 5 1 5 ♭3

11.
1 ♭3 5 ♭3 1

12.
5 ♭3 ♭3 5 1

Diminished

13.
1 ♭5 ♭3 1 1

14.
♭5 ♭3 ♭5 ♭3 1

15.
1 ♭5 1 ♭3 1

Chapter Thirteen

13

Mixed Rhythms

Clap and/or sing the following exercises:

Augmented

Sightsinging—Major Melodies

Sing through the following phrases:

Chapter 13

Chapter Fourteen

14

Mixed Rhythms

Clap and/or sing the following exercises:

INTERVAL WARM-UPS

Complete and sing (ascending intervals):

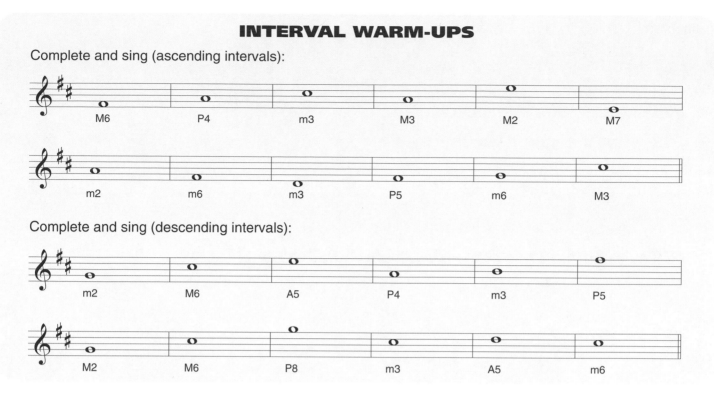

M6 P4 m3 M3 M2 M7

m2 m6 m3 P5 m6 M3

Complete and sing (descending intervals):

m2 M6 A5 P4 m3 P5

M2 M6 P8 m3 A5 m6

Ear Training

For each example, first play through the exercise, listen, and then sing it.

Major

1. 5 1 5 3 1
2. 3 1 1 5 3
3. 3 3 1 1 5

4. 1 5 3 1 5
5. 3 5 3 5 1
6. 1 5 3 5 3

Minor

7. ♭3 1 5 1 ♭3
8. 1 ♭3 5 ♭3 1
9. 1 ♭3 5 ♭3 1

10. 1 ♭3 5 1 ♭3
11. ♭3 1 5 ♭3 5
12. 1 5 ♭3 5 ♭3

Diminished

13. ♭5 1 ♭3 ♭5 ♭3
14. ♭3 ♭5 1 ♭3 ♭5
15. ♭5 ♭3 ♭5 ♭3 1

16. 1 ♭5 1 ♭5 ♭3
17. ♭5 1 ♭5 ♭3 1
18. ♭5 1 ♭5 ♭3 1

Augmented

Sightsinging—Major Melodies

Sing through the following phrases:

Chapter Fifteen

Mixed Rhythms

Clap and/or sing the following exercises:

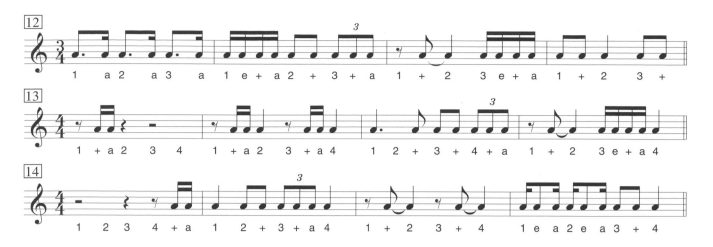

Quarter-Note Triplets

Any time you have triplets, they fit into the same space that two notes of the same value would normally fit. A quarter-note triplet therefore fits into the same space as two quarter notes, or one half note.

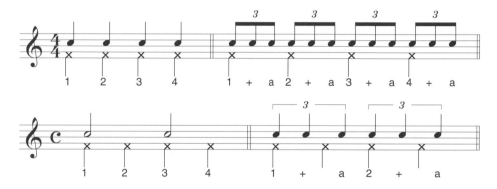

Clap and/or sing the following quarter-note triplet exercises:

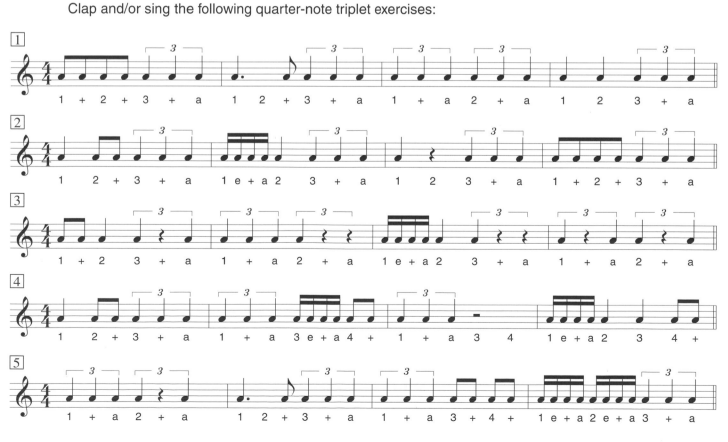

INTERVAL WARM-UPS

Complete and sing (ascending intervals):

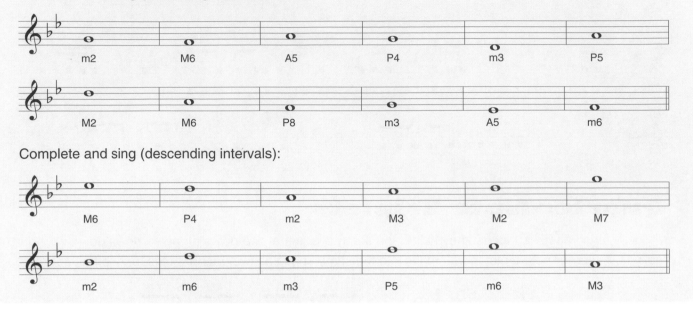

Complete and sing (descending intervals):

Ear Training

For each example, first play through the exercise, listen, and then sing it.

Major

1.   1 3 5 3 1
2.   5 1 3 1 5
3.   3 1 5 3 1
4.   1 3 5 1 3
5.   3 1 5 3 1
6.   1 5 1 3 5

Minor

7.   1 ♭3 5 1 ♭3
8.   ♭3 1 ♭3 5 1
9.   1 5 ♭3 1 ♭3
10.   5 ♭3 1 5 1
11.   ♭3 5 1 ♭3 5
12.   5 1 ♭3 5 1

Diminished

13.   ♭3 1 ♭5 ♭3 1
14.   1 ♭5 ♭3 ♭5 1
15.   ♭3 ♭5 1 ♭3 ♭5
16.   ♭5 1 ♭3 1 ♭5
17.   ♭3 ♭5 1 ♭3 1
18.   1 ♭5 ♭3 ♭5 ♭3

Augmented

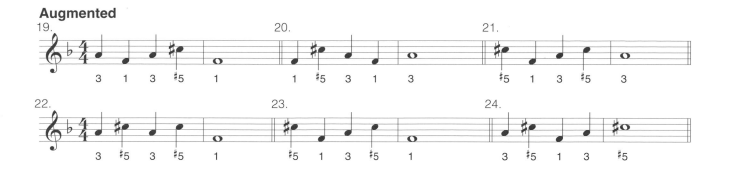

Sightsinging—Major Melodies

Sing through the following phrases:

Chapter Sixteen

16

Mixed Rhythms

Clap and/or sing the following exercises:

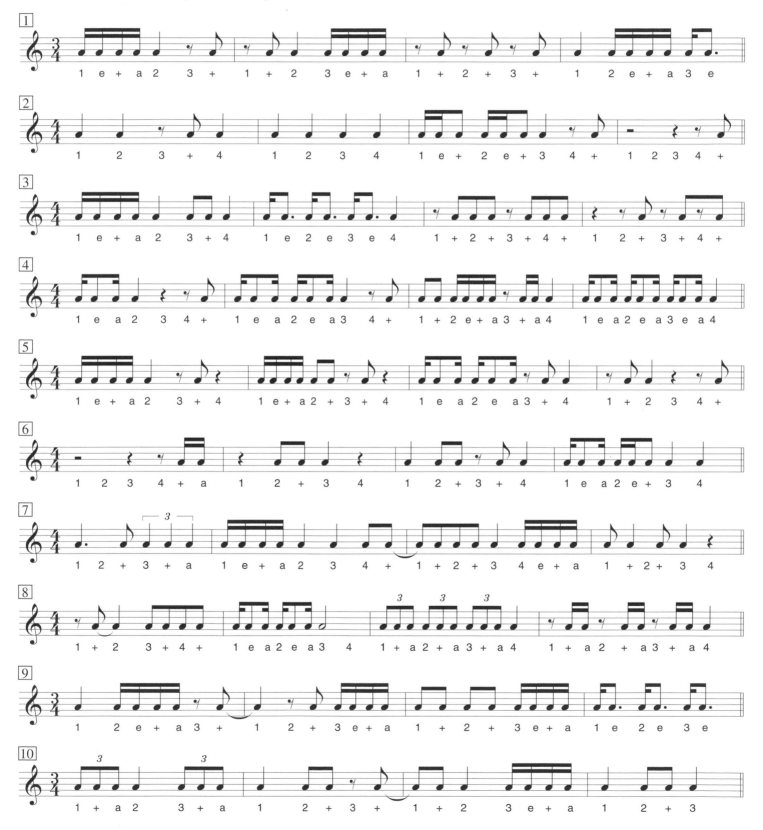

INTERVAL WARM-UPS

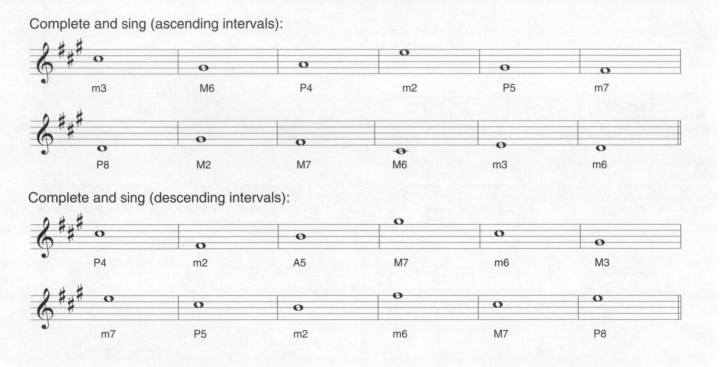

Complete and sing (ascending intervals):

| m3 | M6 | P4 | m2 | P5 | m7 |

| P8 | M2 | M7 | M6 | m3 | m6 |

Complete and sing (descending intervals):

| P4 | m2 | A5 | M7 | m6 | M3 |

| m7 | P5 | m2 | m6 | M7 | P8 |

Seventh Chords

Now that you're familiar with triads, let's move on to the next level, *seventh chords.* Seventh chords are four-note chords. They are essentially triads with the seventh degree added—thus the name "seventh chord." Since there are four notes in a seventh chord, there are more possible combinations than there are for triads. We will look at the five most common types of seventh chords: major seventh, minor seventh, diminished seventh, augmented seventh, and dominant seventh. A *major seventh chord* is a major triad with a major third added on top (the interval of a major seventh from the bottom); a *minor seventh chord* is a minor triad with a minor third added on top (the interval of a minor seventh from the bottom); a *diminished seventh chord* is a diminished triad with a minor third added on top (the interval of a diminished seventh from the bottom); an *augmented seventh chord* is an augmented triad with a diminished third on top (the interval of a minor seventh from the bottom); and a *dominant seventh chord* is a major triad with a minor third added on top (the interval of a minor seventh from the bottom).

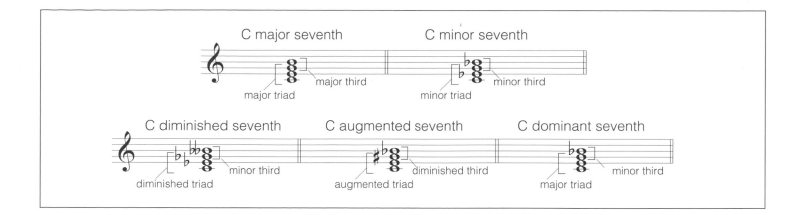

Ear Training

Let's try singing some arpeggiated seventh chords. For each example, first play through the exercise, listen, and then sing it.

Sightsinging—Major Melodies

Sing through the following phrases:

Chapter Seventeen

17

Mixed Rhythms

Clap and/or sing the following exercises:

1 e + a 2   3 + 4   1 + a 2 + a 3   4 +   1   2 + 3 e 4 e   1 e + a 2 + 3 + 4

INTERVAL WARM-UPS

Complete and sing (ascending intervals):

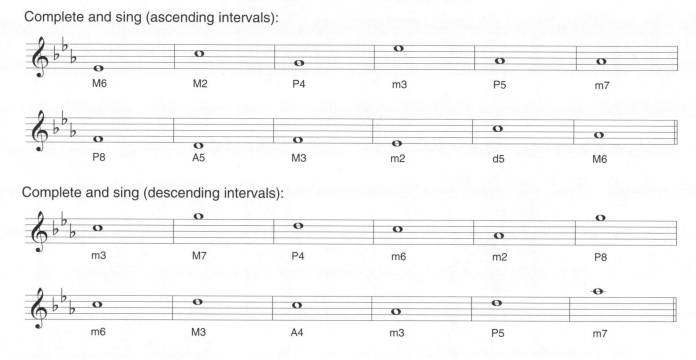

Complete and sing (descending intervals):

Ear Training

For each example, first play through the exercise, listen, and then sing it.

Major 7th

Minor 7th

Dim. 7th

13.

1 ♭3 ♭5 ♭♭7 1

14.

♭5 1 ♭♭7 ♭3 1

15.

1 ♭♭7 ♭3 ♭5 1

16.

1 ♭5 ♭3 ♭♭7 1

Aug. 7th

17.

1 #5 3 ♭7 1

18.

3 ♭7 1 #5 3

19.

3 #5 ♭7 3 1

20.

1 3 ♭7 #5 3

Dom. 7th

21.

1 3 ♭7 5 1

22.

5 ♭7 1 3 1

23.

♭7 3 5 ♭7 1

24.

3 5 ♭7 3 1

Sightsinging—Major Melodies

Sing through the following phrases:

1

1 2 3 5 6 5 4 3 2 1 7 1 2 3 4 5 1

2

3 2 1 7 6 7 2 1 3 5 4 3 2 3 4 5 1

3

5 3 7 1 2 3 4 5 6 5 2 5 6 7 1 2 1 7 7 1

4

3 4 5 4 3 2 3 2 1 7 1 3 4 5 6 7 1

5

1 1 7 6 5 6 5 4 3 4 3 5 7 1 7 1

6

3 4 5 6 5 1 7 6 5 4 3 4 5 6 7 1 2 1

7

3 4 5 4 5 6 7 1 2 1 6 5 4 5 4 3 2 1

Chapter Eighteen

18

Mixed Rhythms

Clap and/or sing the following exercises:

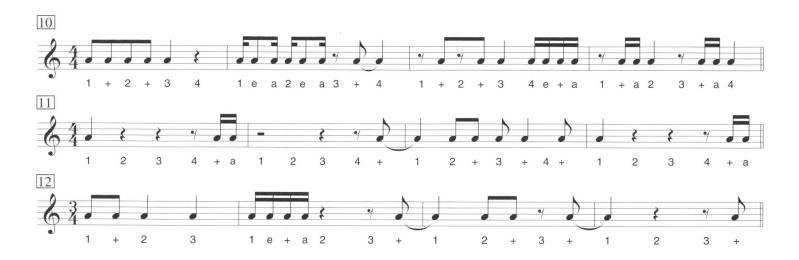

Changing Meters

The following exercises will help familiarize you with changing meters:

INTERVAL WARM-UPS

Complete and sing (ascending intervals):

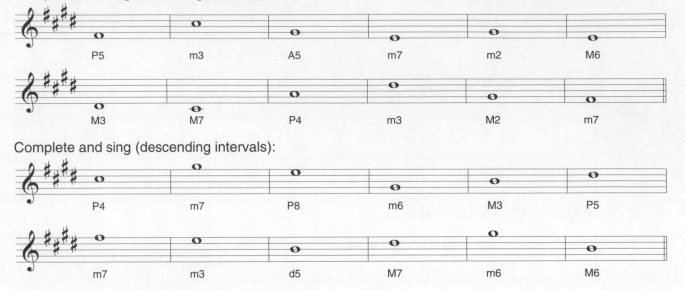

Complete and sing (descending intervals):

Ear Training

For each example, first play through the exercise, listen, and then sing it.

Major 7th

Minor 7th

Dim. 7th

Aug. 7th

Dom. 7th

Sightsinging—Major Melodies

Sing through the following phrases:

Introducing Minor Scales

Natural Minor

The *natural minor* scale is different from the major scale. The third, sixth, and seventh degrees are lowered one half step ascending and descending. These changes in scale degree are incorporated into the key signature. The key signature for C minor is the same as the key signature for E♭ major. Since these two keys have the same signature, C minor is called the *relative minor* of E♭ major.

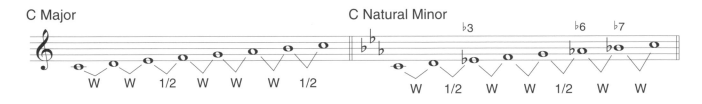

Melodic Minor

The *melodic minor* scale is different from the natural minor scale in that the sixth and seventh degrees are raised one half step ascending. Descending, the melodic minor scale is the same as the natural minor scale—the sixth and seventh degrees are lowered.

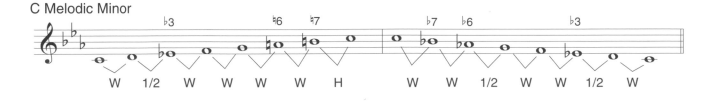

Harmonic Minor

The *harmonic minor* scale is different from the natural minor scale in that the seventh degree is raised one half step (both ascending and descending).

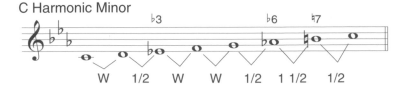

Now let's try singing some minor scale phrases.

1 Natural

2

3

4 Melodic

5

6

7 Harmonic

8

9

Chapter Nineteen

19

Mixed Rhythms

Clap and/or sing the following exercises:

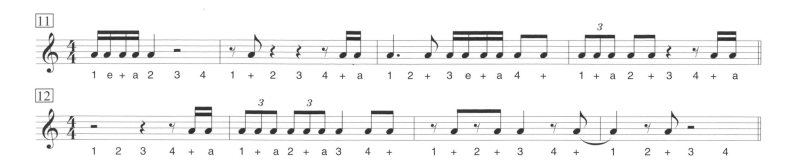

Changing Meters

Clap and/or sing the following changing meter exercises:

INTERVAL WARM-UPS

Complete and sing (ascending intervals):

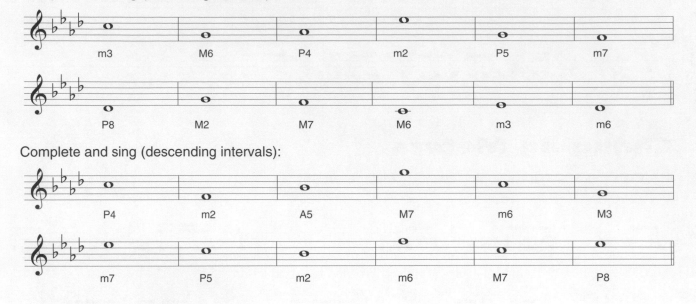

Complete and sing (descending intervals):

Ear Training

For each example, first play through the exercise, listen, and then sing it.

Sightsinging—Major Melodies

Sing through the following major scale phrases:

Minor Melodies

Sing through the following minor scale phrases:

1 **Natural**

Mixed Rhythms

Clap and/or sing the following exercises:

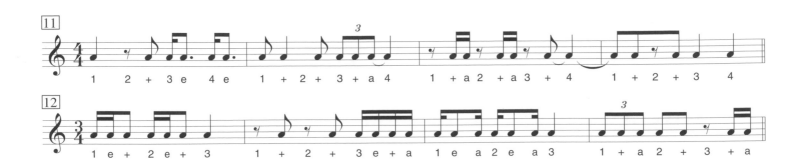

Changing Meters

Clap and/or sing the following changing meter exercises:

INTERVAL WARM-UPS

Complete and sing (ascending intervals):

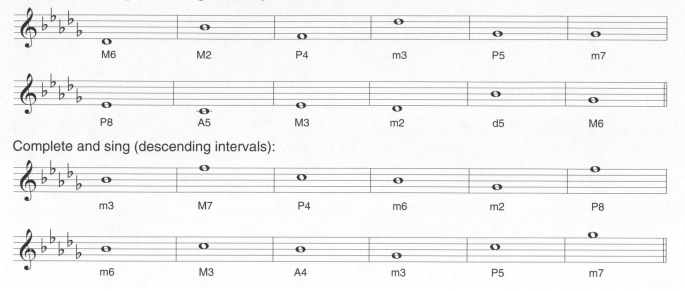

Complete and sing (descending intervals):

Ear Training

For each example, first play through the exercise, listen, and then sing it.

Major 7th

Minor 7th

Dim. 7th

Aug. 7th

Dom. 7th

Sightsinging—Major Melodies

Sing through the following major scale phrases:

Minor Melodies

Sing through the following minor scale phrases:

Chapter Twenty-One
21

Mixed Rhythms

By now, you should no longer need to count the subdivisions out loud. Try to feel the rhythm inside (or count silently in your head) as you read along. Over time, you will find that you aren't counting the subdivisions anymore—you're reading only what's on the page!

INTERVAL WARM-UPS

Complete and sing (ascending intervals):

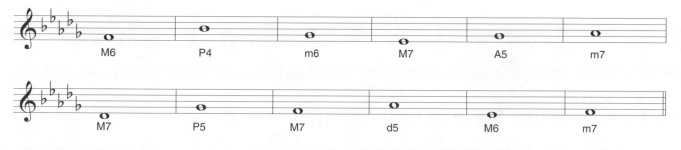

Complete and sing (descending intervals):

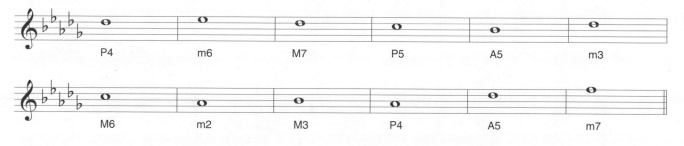

Sightsinging—Major Melodies

By now, you should no longer need to sing the numbers along with the notes. Sing these melodies on "la," or another neutral syllable. Just as you did with the rhythms in the previous exercises, try to connect directly with the pitches inside (or hear them silently in your head just before you sing them) as you read along. Over time you will find that you aren't translating pitches through their numbers—you're reading the notes directly!

Minor Melodies

Sing through the following minor scale phrases:

1 **Natural**

2

3 **Melodic**

4

5 **Harmonic**

6

Two-Part Sightsinging

First, sing through both parts of each exercise separately. Then sing one part while someone else sings the other. Finally, trade parts with each other. If you don't have anyone to sing with, then play one of the parts on a keyboard while you sing the other.

Ear Training

Now we will try singing through phrases created with seventh chord arpeggios.

Chapter Twenty-Two

Mixed Rhythms

Clap and/or sing the following exercises:

INTERVAL WARM-UPS

Complete and sing (ascending intervals):

Complete and sing (descending intervals):

New Chords

Now that you're familiar with triads and four types of seventh chords, we'll introduce three new chords: the minor-major seventh, the minor seventh flat-five, and the dominant seventh flat-nine. A *minor-major seventh chord* is a minor triad with the major seventh degree added. A *minor seventh flat-five chord* is a diminished triad with the minor seventh degree added. A *dominant seventh flat-nine chord* is a dominant chord with a flatted ninth degree added (one octave and one half step above the bottom note).

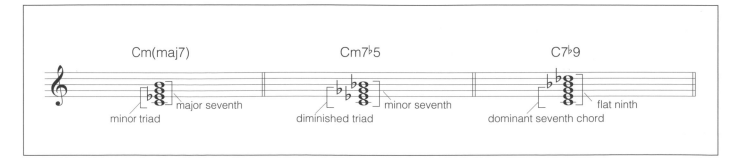

Ear Training

Now let's try singing arpeggiated versions of these new chords. For each example, first play through the exercise, listen, and then sing it.

i(maj7)

ii7♭5

V7♭9

Sightsinging—Major Melodies

Sing through the following major scale phrases:

Minor Melodies

Sing through the following minor scale phrases:

1 **Natural**

2

3 **Melodic**

4

5 **Harmonic**

6

Two-Part Sightsinging

First, sing through both parts of each exercise separately. Then sing the complete exercise with a partner or your own keyboard accompaniment.

Chapter Twenty-Three

23

Mixed Rhythms

Clap and/or sing the following exercises:

INTERVAL WARM-UPS

Complete and sing (ascending intervals):

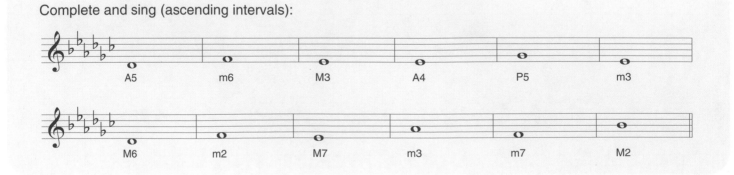

Complete and sing (descending intervals):

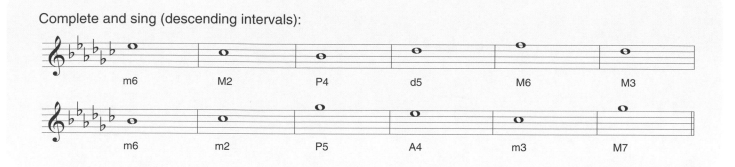

Ear Training

Here are some longer ear training exercises. For each example, first play through the exercise, listen, and then sing it.

Sightsinging—Major Melodies

Sing through the following major scale phrases:

Minor Melodies

Sing through the following minor scale phrases:

1 **Natural**

2

3 **Melodic**

4

5 **Harmonic**

6

Two-Part Sightsinging

First, sing through both parts of each exercise separately, then with a partner or your own keyboard accompaniment.

1

2

3

4

5

6

Chapter Twenty-Four

24

Mixed Rhythms

Clap and/or sing the following exercises:

INTERVAL WARM-UPS

Complete and sing (ascending intervals):

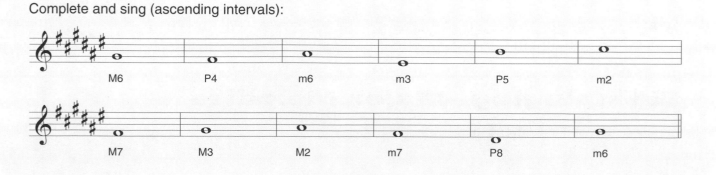

Complete and sing (descending intervals):

Ear Training

For each example, first play through the exercise, listen, and then sing it.

1   Cm(maj7)

2

3   Dm7♭5

4

5   G7♭9

6

Sightsinging—Major Melodies

Sing through the following major scale phrases:

1

Minor Melodies

Sing through the following minor scale phrases:

Two-Part Sightsinging

First sing through each part separately, then with another singer or your own keyboard accompaniment.

3

4 **D Natural Minor**

5 **D Melodic Minor**

6 **D Harmonic Minor**

Chapter Twenty-Five

25

Mixed Rhythms

Clap and/or sing the following exercises:

INTERVAL WARM-UPS

In this chapter, we'll begin exploring chromatic intervals in our interval warm-ups. Sing through the following two exercises, using "la" or a similar neutral syllable:

Ear Training

For each example, first play through the exercise, listen, and then sing it.

Sightsinging—Major Melodies

Sing through the following major scale phrases:

Minor Melodies

Sing through the following minor scale phrases:

Two-Part Sightsinging

First sing through each part separately, then with another singer or your own keyboard accompaniment.

2

3

4

5

6

Chapter Twenty-Six

26

Mixed Rhythms

Clap and/or sing the following exercises:

INTERVAL WARM-UPS

Sing through the following large interval exercises:

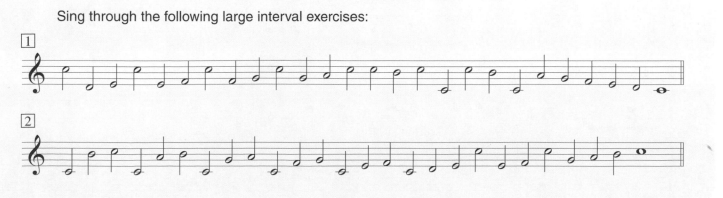

Ear Training

For each example, first play through the exercise, listen, and then sing it.

Sightsinging—Major Melodies

Sing through the following major scale phrases:

Minor Melodies

Sing through the following minor scale phrases:

Two-Part Sightsinging

First sing through each part separately, then with another singer or your own keyboard accompaniment.

Chapter Twenty-Seven

Mixed Rhythms

Clap and/or sing the following exercises:

Ear Training

For each example, first play through the exercise, listen, and then sing it.

Sightsinging—Major Melodies

Sing through the following major scale phrases:

Minor Melodies

Sing through the following minor scale phrases:

The Blues Scale

The blues scale is constructed of two whole steps, two half steps, and two minor thirds. The location of the whole steps, half steps, and minor thirds are shown below.

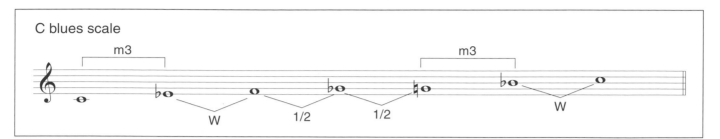

Sing through the following blues scale phrases:

Two-Part Sightsinging—Minor

First sing through each part separately, then with another singer or your own keyboard accompaniment.

1 **Natural**

2

3 Melodic

4

5 Harmonic

6

Chapter Twenty-Eight

28

Mixed Rhythms

Clap and/or sing the following exercises:

Ear Training

For each example, first play through the exercise, listen, and then sing it.

Sightsinging—Major Melodies

Sing through the following major scale phrases:

Minor Melodies

Sing through the following minor scale phrases:

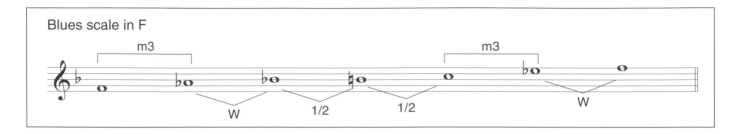

Blues Melodies

Sing through the following blues scale phrases:

Two-Part Sightsinging—Minor

First sing through each part separately, then with another singer or your own keyboard accompaniment.

3 Melodic

4

5 Harmonic

6

Chapter Twenty-Nine

29

Mixed Rhythms

Clap and/or sing the following exercises:

Ear Training

For each example, first play through the exercise, listen, and then sing it.

Sightsinging—Major Melodies

Sing through the following major scale phrases:

Minor Melodies

Sing through the following minor scale phrases:

1 **Natural**

2 **Melodic**

3 **Harmonic**

Modes

A *mode* is formed by taking a scale and, instead of starting on the tonic (I), starting from any other note in the scale and playing up to the same note an octave higher.

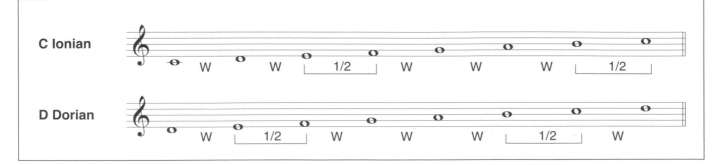

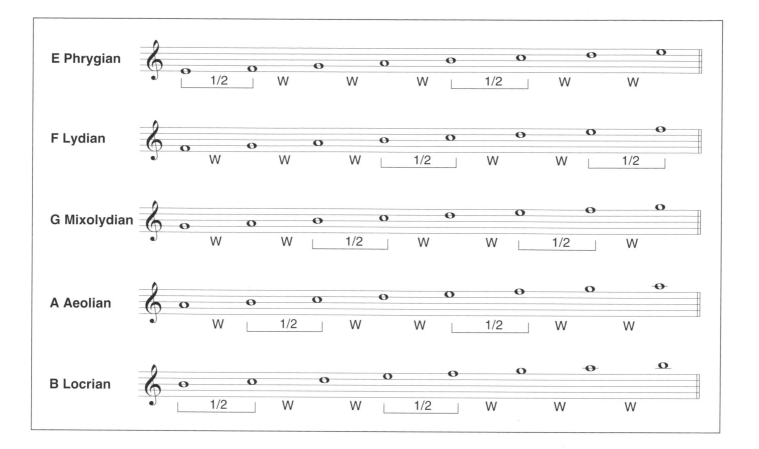

Now let's try singing through some modal phrases:

1 Dorian

2

3 Phrygian

4

5 Lydian

6

7 Mixolydian

8

9 Aeolian

10

11 Locrian

12

Chapter Thirty

Mixed Rhythms

Clap and/or sing the following exercises:

Ear Training

For each example, first play through the exercise, listen, and then sing it.

Sightsinging—Major Melodies

Sing through the following major scale phrases:

Minor Melodies

Sing through the following minor scale phrases:

"Putting It on the Line"

There comes a time when you get your first call for a session. It might be a song demo, a jingle for a major car company, a movie or television soundtrack where you would be asked to sing the title song, a background session for Sting, or just going over to some friends' house to record an original song of theirs on a four-track machine. Someone hands you a piece of sheet music, and they say, "Look this over... We'll start in a few minutes!!!"

The panic begins. You start sweating. Can you do this? Well, if you've practiced hard, and you've gotten to the end of Chapter 30, the answer is yes! You *can* do this! You might not be able to sightsing the whole song without a mistake the first time, but you'll be singing the melody and rhythm in your head. You'll hear it, and it will make sense. The panic will start to leave, and your confidence will begin to show. You *can* do this.

Most of the professional singers and instrumentalists I have known and worked with in my career have always said that a session is 95% boredom and 5% sheer terror. To help give you a concept of what you might encounter along the road, I've included here a few lead sheets, a short jingle, and some vocal group insanity. Remember, if you can really sing, have good ears, can read music fairly well, and have a professional attitude and a strong desire, a lot of doors will open for you. Time is money. People want it done well, and they want it done fast.

Good luck, and keep singing!

SONG 1
Ya Got Me Crazy For Your Love
WORDS & MUSIC BY TOM PETERSON AND MIKE CAMPBELL

SONG 2
I Love You, in 3/4 Time
Words & Music by Mike Campbell A.S.C.A.P.

VERSE 3: SHE'S SO FUNKY, SHE'S SO CLASSY, SHE CAN SING LIKE
SHIRLEY BASSEY. SHE'S GOOD MORNING WITH
BREAKFAST IN BED, SHE'S A BLIZZARD IN OCTOBER,
I HAVE FOUND MY FOUR LEAF CLOVER.
SHE'S AS SEDUCTIVE AS A WARM WATER BED.

SONG 3
THE CITY
WORDS & MUSIC BY MIKE CAMPBELL A.S.C.A.P.

SONG 4
JINGLE

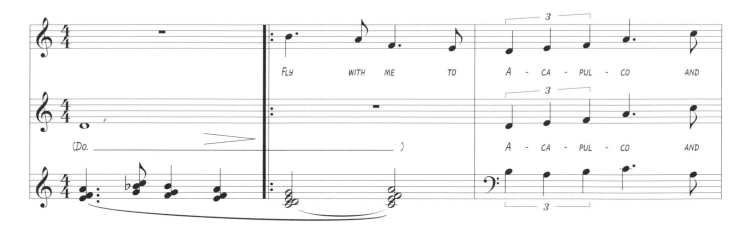

SONG 5
VOCAL GROUP INSANITY

Voice Ranges

Know the different voice ranges and how they fit on the grand staff.

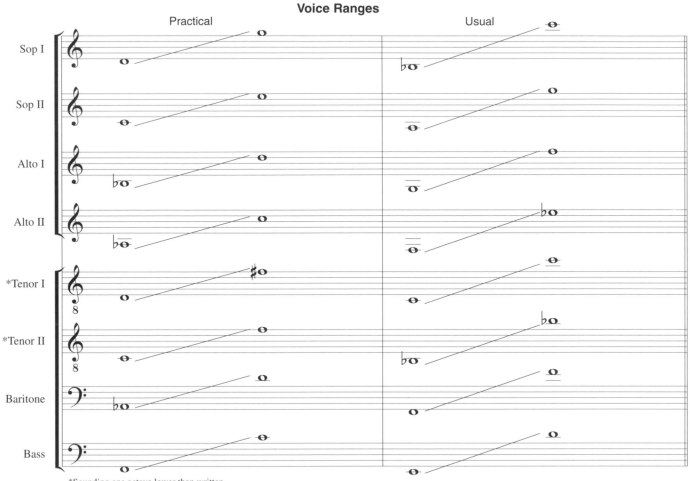

Voice Ranges

*Sounding one octave lower than written

The Grand Staff

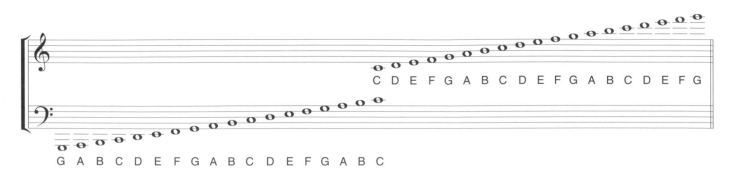

The Circle of Fifths

The *circle of fifths* is a useful tool for memorizing both major and minor keys and their key signatures. Proceeding clockwise around the circle, you move through keys in fifths (e.g., C–G–D–A–E–B–etc.), adding a sharp with each key signature. Proceeding counterclockwise, you move through the keys in fourths (e.g., C–F–B♭–E♭–A♭–D♭–etc.), adding a flat with each signature.

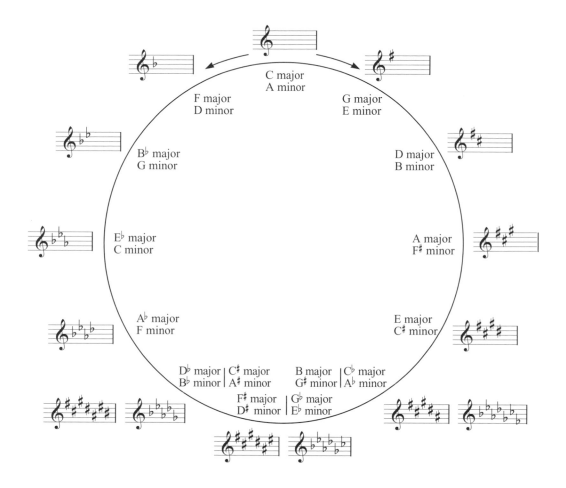

Order of sharps – F C G D A E B

Order of flats   – B E A D G C F

(Notice how the order of sharps and flats
are mirror images of each other!)

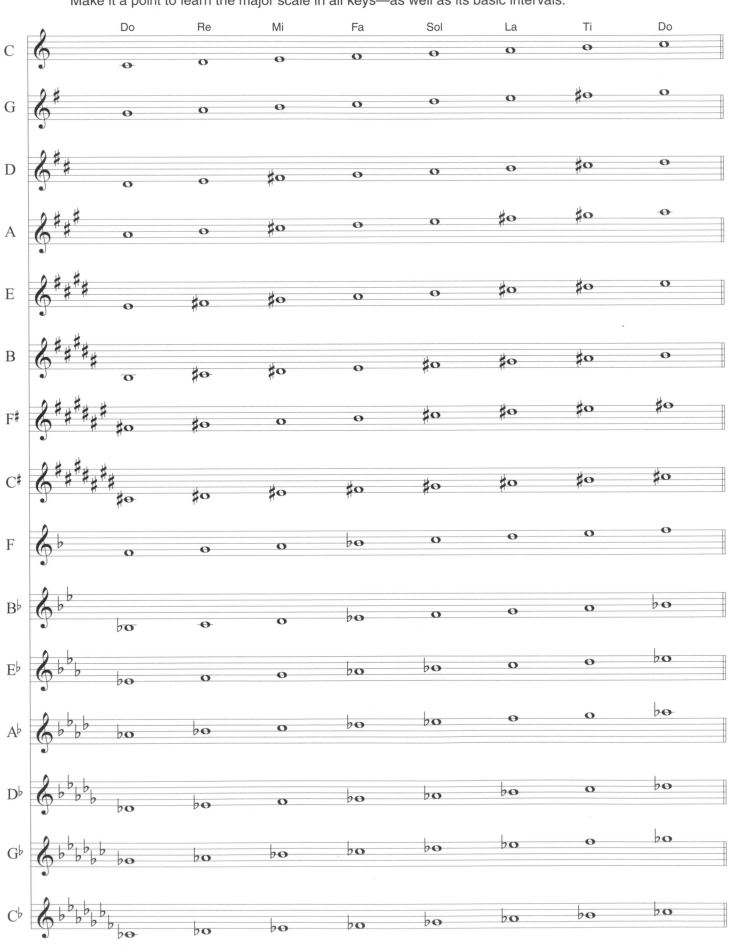

Major Scales in All Keys

Make it a point to learn the major scale in all keys—as well as its basic intervals.

Basic Major Scale Intervals

Scales

Here are most of the scales you'll likely come in contact with during your musical life.

Chromatic	P1	m2	M2	m3	M3	P4	A4/d5	P5	m6	M6	m7	M7	P8
Major (Ionian)	1		2		3	4		5		6		7	8
Dorian	1		2	♭3		4		5		6	♭7		8
Phrygian	1	♭2		♭3		4		5	♭6		♭7		8
Lydian	1		2		3		♯4	5		6		7	8
Mixolydian	1		2		3	4		5		6	♭7		8
Natural Minor (Aeolian)	1		2	♭3		4		5	♭6		♭7		8
Harmonic Minor	1		2	♭3		4		5	♭6			7	8
Melodic Minor (*ascend.*)	1		2	♭3		4		5		6		7	8
Melodic Minor (*descend.*)	1		2	♭3		4		5	♭6		♭7		8
Locrian	1	♭2		♭3		4	♭5		♭6		♭7		8
Blues	1			♭3		4	♯4/♭5	5			♭7		8
Major Pentatonic	1		2		3			5		6			8
Minor Pentatonic	1			♭3		4		5			♭7		8
Whole Tone (*ascend.*)	1		2		3		♯4		♯5		♯6		8
Whole Tone (*descend.*)	1		2		3		♭5		♭6		♭7		8
Overtone	1		2		3		♯4	5		6	♭7		8
Diminished (W/H)	1		2	♭3		4	♭5		♭6	6		7	8
Diminished (H/W)	1	♭2		♭3	3		♭5	5		6	♭7		8

(The column header shows a "Whole" step bracket spanning m2–M2 and a "Half" step bracket spanning P1–m2.)

About the Author

VIT's program director, Mike Campbell has recorded six solo albums and CDs. His voice has been heard in many jingles, TV and movie soundtracks, and he has opened for and performed with the likes of Ella Fitzgerald, Sarah Vaughn, Benny Carter, Count Basie, Henry Mancini, and Nancy Wilson. Also an actor, Mike has appeared on camera for several major commercials and has sung on over forty television shows.

Mike has served on the Board of Governors of N.A.R.A.S. and is a member of A.F. of M., S.A.G., A.F.T.R.A., A.S.C.A.P., and I.A.J.E. He has performed in concerts, jazz festivals, and clinics across the United States, Europe, and Australia, is the co-author of *Harmony Vocals,* also available from Hal Leonard Corporation.

MUSICIANS INSTITUTE ™

Musicians Institute Press is the official series of instructional publications from Southern California's renowned music school, Musicians Institute. These books, book/audio packages, and videos have been created by MI instructors who are among the world's best and most experienced professional musicians.

KEYBOARD

00695708	Blues Hanon by Peter Deneff	$17.99
00695556	Dictionary of Keyboard Grooves by Gail Johnson – Book/CD	$16.95
00202430	Easy Jazz Hanon by Peter Deneff – Book/Audio	$12.99
00695336	Funk Keyboards – The Complete Method by Gail Johnson – Book/Audio	$16.99
00695936	Hip-Hop Keyboard by Henry Soleh Brewer – Book/CD	$17.95
00695791	Jazz Chord Hanon by Peter Deneff	$17.99
00695554	Jazz Hanon by Peter Deneff	$16.99
00695773	Jazz Piano by Christian Klikovits – Book/CD	$19.99
00695209	Keyboard Voicings by Kevin King	$12.95
00266448	Modal Hanon by Peter Deneff	$14.99
00145419	Pop Keyboard Concepts by Christian Klikovits – Book/Audio	$19.99
00695509	Pop Rock Keyboards by Henry Sol-Eh Brewer & David Garfield – Book/CD	$19.95
00695784	Rock Hanon by Peter Deneff	$19.99
00695226	Salsa Hanon by Peter Deneff	$17.99
00695939	Samba Hanon by Peter Deneff	$16.99
00695882	Stride Hanon by Peter Deneff	$17.99

VOICE

00695883	Advanced Vocal Technique by Dena Murray and Tita Hutchison – Book/Audio	$19.99
00695262	Harmony Vocals by Mike Campbell & Tracee Lewis – Book/Audio	$19.99
00695626	The Musician's Guide to Recording Vocals by Dallan Beck – Book/CD	$15.99
00695629	Rock Vocals by Coreen Sheehan – Book/CD	$17.99
00695195	Sightsinging by Mike Campbell	$19.99
00695427	Vocal Technique by Dena Murray – Book/Audio	$24.99

GUITAR

00695922	Acoustic Artistry by Evan Hirschelman – Book/Audio	$19.99
00695298	Advanced Scale Concepts and Licks for Guitar by Jean Marc Belkadi – Book/CD	$17.99
00217709	All-in-One Guitar Soloing Course by Daniel Gilbert & Beth Marlis	$29.99
00695132	Blues Guitar Soloing by Keith Wyatt – Book/Online Media	$24.99
00695680	Blues/Rock Soloing for Guitar by Robert Calva – Book/Audio	$19.99
00695131	Blues Rhythm Guitar by Keith Wyatt – Book/Audio	$19.99
00696002	Modern Techniques for the Electric Guitarist by Dean Brown – DVD	$29.95
00695664	Chord Progressions for Guitar by Tom Kolb – Book/CD	$17.99
00695855	Chord Tone Soloing by Barrett Tagliarino – Book/Audio	$24.99
00695646	Chord-Melody Guitar by Bruce Buckingham – Book/CD	$19.99
00695171	Classical & Fingerstyle Guitar Techniques by David Oakes – Book/Audio	$17.99
00695806	Classical Themes for Electric Guitar by Jean Marc Belkadi – Book/CD	$15.99
00695661	Country Guitar by Al Bonhomme – Book/Audio	$19.99

00695227	The Diminished Scale for Guitar by Jean Marc Belkadi – Book/CD	$14.99
00695181	Essential Rhythm Guitar by Steve Trovato – Book/CD	$15.99
00695873	Ethnic Rhythms for Electric Guitar by Jean Marc Belkadi – Book/CD	$17.99
00695860	Exotic Scales & Licks for Electric Guitar by Jean Marc Belkadi – Book/CD	$16.95
00695419	Funk Guitar by Ross Bolton – Book/Audio	$15.99
00695134	Guitar Basics by Bruce Buckingham – Book/Audio	$17.99
00695712	Guitar Fretboard Workbook by Barrett Tagliarino	$19.99
00695321	Guitar Hanon by Peter Deneff	$14.99
00695482	The Guitar Lick•tionary by Dave Hill – Book/CD	$19.99
00695190	Guitar Soloing by Daniel Gilbert and Beth Marlis – Book/Audio	$22.99
00695169	Harmonics by Jamie Findlay – Book/CD	$13.99
00695406	Introduction to Jazz Guitar Soloing by Joe Elliott – Book/Audio	$19.95
00695291	Jazz Guitar Chord System by Scott Henderson	$12.99
00217711	Jazz Guitar Improvisation by Sid Jacobs – Book/Online Media	$19.99
00217690	Jazz, Rock & Funk Guitar by Dean Brown – Book/Online Media	$19.99
00695361	Jazz-Rock Triad Improvising for Guitar by Jean Marc Belkadi – Book/CD	$15.99
00695379	Latin Guitar by Bruce Buckingham – Book/Audio	$17.99
00696656	Liquid Legato by Allen Hinds – Book/CD	$14.99
00695143	A Modern Approach to Jazz, Rock & Fusion Guitar by Jean Marc Belkadi – Book/CD	$15.99
00695711	Modern Jazz Concepts for Guitar by Sid Jacobs – Book/CD	$16.95
00695682	Modern Rock Rhythm Guitar by Danny Gill – Book/CD	$16.95
00695555	Modes for Guitar by Tom Kolb – Book/Audio	$18.99
00695192	Music Reading for Guitar by David Oakes	$19.99
00695697	Outside Guitar Licks by Jean Marc Belkadi – Book/CD	$16.99
00695962	Power Plucking by Dale Turner – Book/CD	$19.95
00695748	Progressive Tapping Licks by Jean Marc Belkadi – Book/CD	$16.99
00114559	Rhythm Guitar by Bruce Buckingham & Eric Paschal – Book/Audio	$24.99
00695188	Rhythm Guitar by Bruce Buckingham & Eric Paschal – Book	$19.99
00695909	Rhythm Guitar featuring Bruce Buckingham – DVD	$19.95
00110263	Rhythmic Lead Guitar by Barrett Tagliarino – Book/Audio	$19.99
00695144	Rock Lead Basics by Nick Nolan and Danny Gill – Book/Audio	$18.99
00695278	Rock Lead Performance by Nick Nolan and Danny Gill – Book/Audio	$17.99
00695146	Rock Lead Techniques by Nick Nolan and Danny Gill – Book/Audio	$16.99
00695977	Shred Guitar by Greg Harrison – Book/Audio	$19.99
00139556	Solo Slap Guitar by Jude Gold – Book/Video	$19.99
00695645	Slap & Pop Technique for Guitar by Jean Marc Belkadi – Book/CD	$16.99
00695913	Technique Exercises for Guitar by Jean Marc Belkadi – Book/CD	$15.99
00695340	Texas Blues Guitar by Robert Calva – Book/Audio	$17.99
00695863	Ultimate Guitar Technique by Bill LaFleur – Book/Audio	$22.99